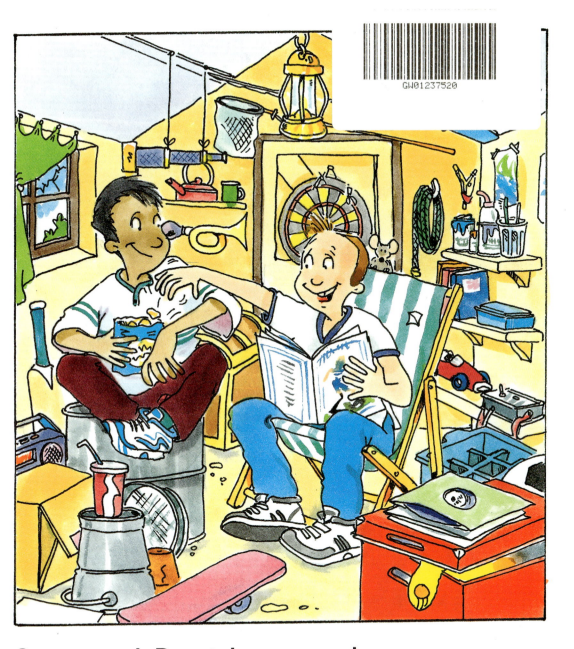

Sam and Ravi have a den.

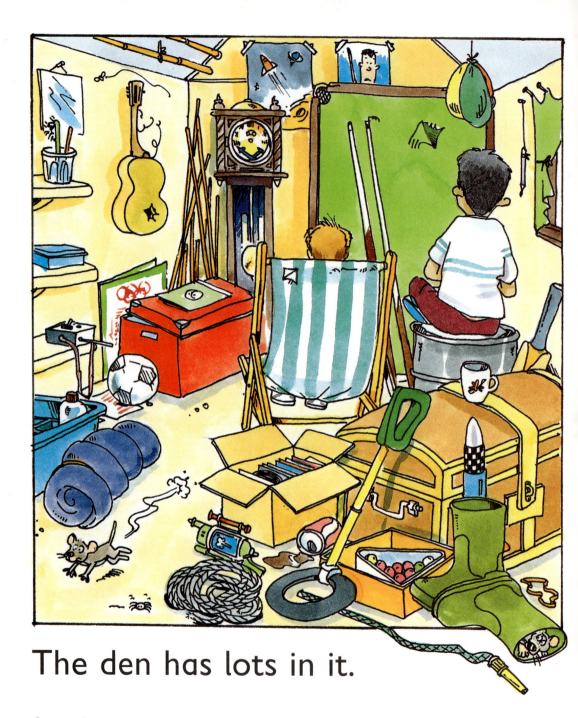

The den has lots in it.

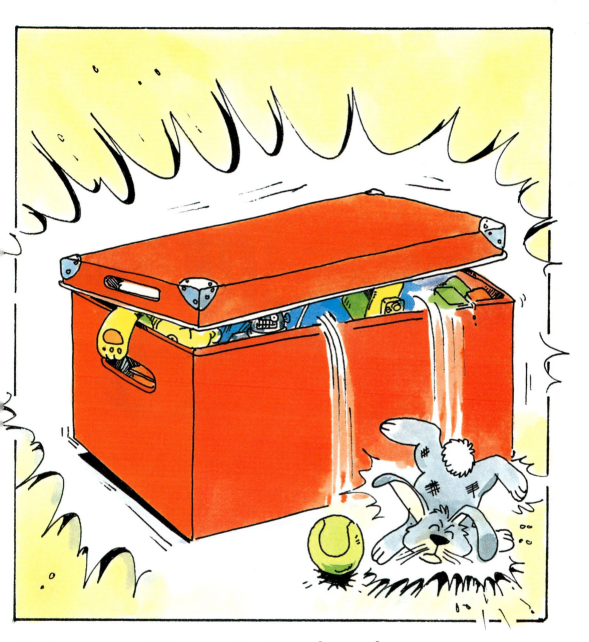

A big red box is in the den.

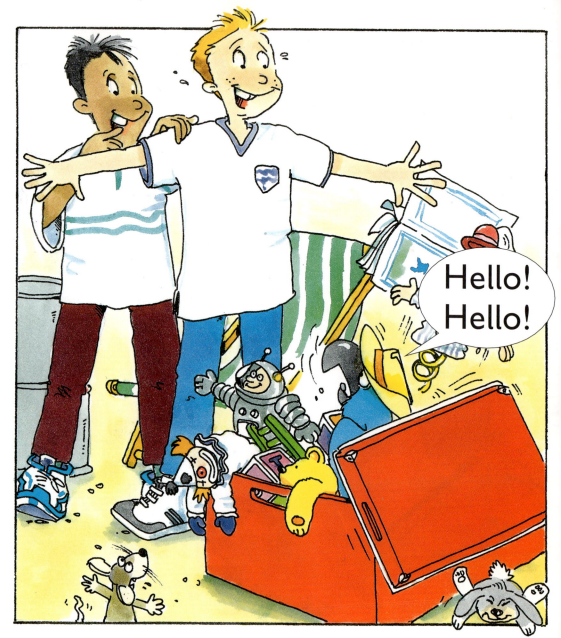

Mrs Cherry's parrot is in the box!

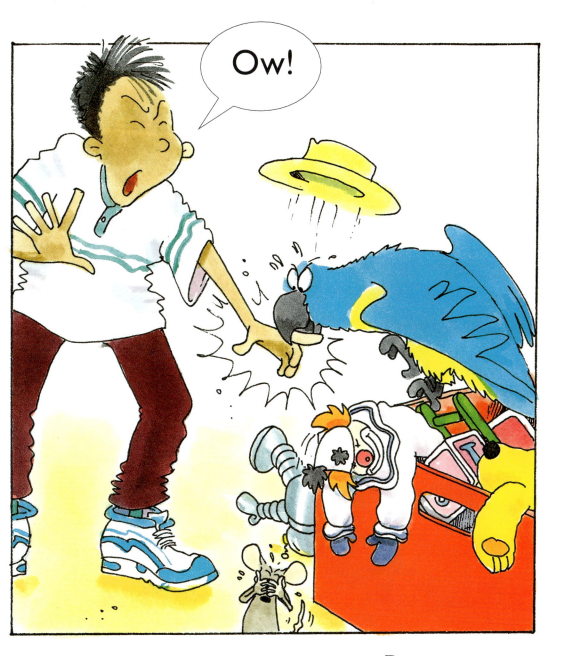

The naughty parrot nips Ravi.

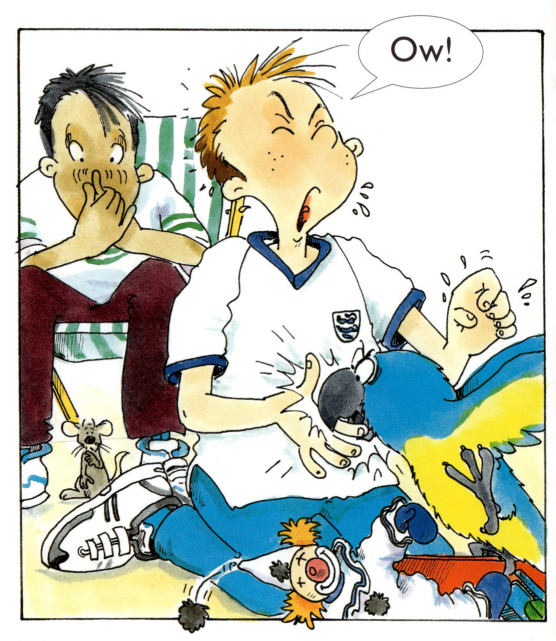

The naughty parrot nips Sam!

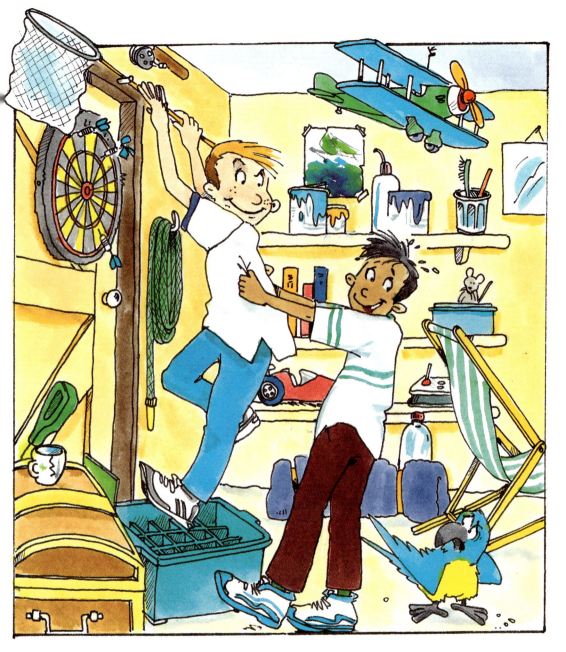

Sam and Ravi get a big net.

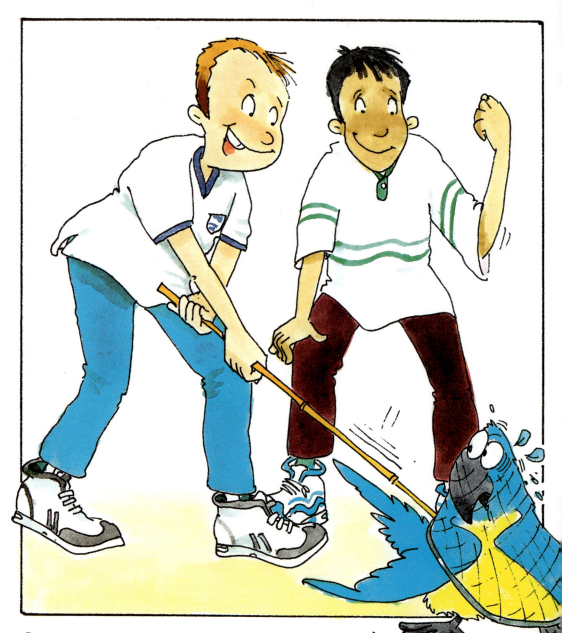

Sam nets the parrot!